# YOUR USER'S MANUAL

A Guide for Purpose and an Anxiety
Free Life in the 21st Century

ANDERSON SILVER

# CONTENTS

# PREFACE

About the dogmas and rules of living a good life:

> "It is about this that philosophers ought to meditate; this is what they should write down every day, and it should be the subject of their exercises."
>
> — Marcus Aurelius

The following pages are a collection of teachings that has helped me attain a level of tranquility that I never thought previously possible. Although the main influences are, as the reader will notice, Stoicism and the Buddha Dharma (Buddha's teachings, not to be confused with Buddhism), the ideas come from many branches of philosophy and science. A core practice of the Stoic way of life is repetition of the good dogmas, to replace the old ones that cause angst and anxiety.

> "You must have these principles at hand both night and day; you must write them down; you must read them."
>
> — Marcus Aurelius

These collections of thoughts that follow were initially my meditations, a handy guide to refer to and periodically read regarding my established rules, or dogmas, for life. Their purpose was to remind myself all the creeds of leading a tranquil life, and through repetitive reading to keep the old bad perspectives at bay. The following book morphed from these meditations. I had shared my meditations with a troubled soul and a listening ear. Following good feedback and positive results from this person close to my heart, I decided to turn the entirety of my meditations into a user friendly book, in the hopes that it may help a great many more people with *listening ears* find their inner peace and their way to a tranquil life in this modern, hectic world we live in.

As it was initially written for myself, I would like to present the reader with a few definitions for the purpose of clarity of the text. For example, when I refer to *meditation*, it is not necessarily the Buddhist mindful concentration meditation. Reading, reflecting and writing about a specific topic is typically what I consider my meditation. Although the mindful concentration meditation is also very useful, helpful and recommended, for the purposes of philosophy *meditation* refers to reflecting on ideas, not just oneself or peacefulness.

There are many references to *virtue* or lack thereof, as virtue is a core element of Stoicism. This virtue more specifically refers to honesty, honourability, and the rational mind. The rational ordinary mind is also an important distinction to make, as the ordinary mind refers to a mind devoid of and free from emotions.

Another important definition is that of happiness. In the daily colloquial language, we tend to use happiness in two ways:
1. To indicate elation and joy.
2. To describe a mental and emotional state of well-being.

The following thoughts will vehemently reject happiness. This rejection refers to the first definition (above) of the word, in the form of an emotional high of elation or joy. The following collection of thoughts' ultimate goal is to, in fact, help you get to and stay at, the second definition of the word.

I also encourage the reader to read the following thoughts with an open mind. Understand the concepts and the logic behind them that have withstood the test of time. But then question them. Question everything. However, remind yourself first, that one cannot question something they do not fully understand.

Finally, this book is meant to inspire a new outlook on life, not to offer a concrete or complete framework of actions and behaviors. And so I encourage the reader to see beyond the words and embrace their message. Should you chose to begin a new approach to life, consider this as your very first step and know that there will be many more to come.

# 1 BECOMING A PHILOSOPHER KING

Congratulations, you are alive. This means you share the same unfortunate condition with 7.6 billion other people: The Human Condition. You did not ask to be here, yet you were given life and consciousness. You were also given a death sentence. What's more is you were not given a purpose or a reason. You just are with an unknown yet unavoidable expiration date. This is at best a confusing circumstance, and at worse a scary and depressing condition. Why am I here, you wonder? Why must I suffer and what is the purpose of life?

You work for the weekend. You look forward to vacations. You think about the events and gatherings you will attend with loved ones, friends and family for a happy and enjoyable time. You look forward to your alone time or relax time when you get home at night. You tolerate the drudgery of your day-to-day to enjoy those few moments in life when you can be free and happy (of which you never seem to get enough). You live with anxiety, fear everything, and find life to be difficult and unfair all too often. Why can't it be easy? Such is life, right?

Not really. Are you content with living a miserable or barely tolerable life most of the time so as to be able to enjoy few and far between happy moments? Sounds more like a prison sentence than an enjoyable life. You ask yourself, "Why can't I be in a good place all the time, instead of sacrificing most of my time to have some good moments in life?" Many have asked this question before you, including the ancient philosophers of Greece and Rome. And if they got it right, there is a way to be permanently in a good headspace: Become a philosopher king.

As a philosopher king, you can be in a good place all the time, whether you are working, playing, eating, meditating, walking, are sick, healthy, on vacation, in jail or even while being tortured physically or mentally. A philosopher king is always in a good place regardless of where he is, what he is doing, or what is happening around him. This sounds like a good deal – after all, you do not want pain or suffering, so why not follow the guidelines of the ancient philosophers to become a philosopher king? If there is a condition whereby you can live your life the way you truly want to, free of suffering, would you not pursue said condition with the utmost urgency? Living a tranquil life, where you remain in a good place regardless of the world that seems to want to punish you at every pass, is something to be desired.

In 2010, the San José mine in Chile collapsed trapping 33 men 2300 feet underground. As they laid there hungry and thirsty in the hot damp darkness for 16 days without any contact from the surface above, they prepared for death. A few of the miners began talking about how they would change their lives and live it the way they want to should they miraculously get a second lease on life. After 69 days of being trapped they were rescued and they did change the way they lived their lives. But why did they need a brush with death to begin living their lives in harmony instead of going about it confused and unhappy? If they had it in them the whole time, why did they not already live their lives in an anxiety free manner? Why were they waiting? The more pressing question is, why are you waiting?

# 2 THE JOURNEY

The truth is that you cannot become a philosopher king any more than you can levitate through meditation. The freedom and tranquility you will obtain come from not the destination, but the journey. Live every day by a set of rules, mantras, and dogma and work your way toward becoming a philosopher king. This is your salvation.

There is no condition in which one can be happy all the time. In the same way, there is no condition where one can be sad all the time. One cannot always be in happy moments. The repetitive happy moment would then become a normal state. Then you need to up the ante and do something more to be happier. Then more, and more, until there is nothing better and so you end up in depression. With ups, inevitably there are downs and vice versa. Without the sad times, one cannot have happy times as one would not even know what they are. This cycle of the Yin and Yang is unavoidable, so how can we possibly pursue a happy life, if sadness is inevitable? The simple answer is that we cannot.

Emotions, by their nature, come and go. They are fleeting. Therefore pursuing a life based on chasing an emotion, such as happiness, necessarily obliges that at certain times you simply cannot attain your pursued emotion. In other words, by setting an emotion as your objective, you immediately must accept that you will fail your objective some or most of the time. To pursue something that you can only get some of the time, and to base your life on it, is a fool's errand. Therefore the pursuit must necessarily be about something else, something more.

Along with emotions, you also have a state of mind. You feel anxieties. To worry about the unknown, for example, when and how you will die, can cause anxiety. It can also be consistent and last a lifetime, as there are many unknowns and there always will be. Unlike emotions that have no state where they can exist consistently and forever, anxiety as a state of mind does have conditions where it can exist permanently. Therefore, there is also a way of living where you can have a state of mind whereby you are free of anxiety: Tranquility.

Accordingly, the lifelong journey to become a philosopher king is not for the purpose of pursuing happiness, but it is the pursuit of Tranquility. The pursuit of a Tranquil life will liberate you from fear and anxiety, regardless of how "good" or "bad" life and the world around you appears to be.

# 3 YOU ARE NOT SPECIAL

In quantum physics, quarks[1] go in and out of existence (or rather from our dimension). When matter and antimatter appear at the same time and pair up, they cancel each other out and disappear. Right before the Big Bang, in the grand scale, there would have been about equal amounts of matter and antimatter. However, at any given time, there may be some small amount of quarks in existence (in our dimension) waiting for antiquarks to appear so that they may pair up and annihilate each other. This also happens vice-versa in that there may be pockets of antiquarks that lay around waiting to be paired up. 13.8 billion years ago, as matter and antimatter were popping in and out of existence, the Big Bang, fueled by the minor amounts of quarks floating around began the expansion of our

---

[1] *Quarks are the smallest particles of matter that we have discovered to date.*

universe. From this minuscule amount of leftover quarks, our entire visible universe was created. This visible universe stretches 93 billion light-years across and was made up of a minor amount of quarks that were waiting around for their anti-quarks. These are truly cosmic and humbling scales. A beam of light, the fastest thing known to us, would take 93 billion years to traverse the visible universe. Compared to little ol' you, the universe is colossal.

Now consider yourself and your significance within the universe. To say you are small in the cosmic scale of things is a gross overstatement. Think about the sheer quantity of events that must have occurred in the history of this giant, vast 13.8 billion-year-old universe. You have been around for a handful of years, and at maturity might make it past a century. That means you are a participant in $7.25 \times 10^{-9}\%$ or $0.00000000725\%$ of the known life of the visible part of the universe. In other words, a totally and utterly insignificant part of the universe in the cosmic scale of things.

But you are a Homo Sapiens, the crown jewel of the universe, no? Not quite so. For starters, if we have life on this planet, that means the universe contains the building block for life. With the universe's scale, size and longevity, it is a statistical certainty that life exists elsewhere, always has existed, and always will as long as the universe is around and doing its thing. The fact that we have not yet detected life elsewhere has more to do with our lack of technological capabilities, then it has to do with the question of life existing elsewhere in the universe.

From a philosophical perspective, to think life is unique to our small and unassuming planet, circling a relatively common star, would be to ignore the simple fact that we come from stardust, and that stardust is abundant everywhere in the universe. It would also ignore the fact that the rules of the universe are consistent and the same everywhere. And so with stardust everywhere and the laws of the universe being the same everywhere, life must also be everywhere, must have been around for a long time, and will still be for a long time to come.

Even if we were to have the delusion that life is unique to our planet, as a species we are one of the most unsuccessful animals to ever roam it. Every other animal has learned to live with its environment and survived for long periods of time. The dinosaurs existed for 165 million years. The shark has been around for 425 million years. The collective human species (genus homo[2]) has been around for a mere 2 million years and we have been nothing but destructive, causing more deaths and extinctions than any other predator.

But we're Homo Sapiens (the word *Sapiens* coming from the Latin word for *Wise*). We built cities, we developed advanced technologies, we built rockets and explored space. We have

---

[2] *Some more commonly known human species are Homo Neanderthalensis (commonly referred to as Neanderthals) and Homo Erectus (the most successful of any human species in terms of longevity). However, in recent years many more discoveries have been made of other different extinct human species, including Homo Floresiensis, who lived on an island in Indonesia and adults grew to a height of only 3 feet.*

modern medicine and cars and flying machines and the Internet. We have achieved so much, we must be important or special in some way? Do not deceive yourself. Even among all the different human species, we, Homo Sapiens, are the most destructive and shortsighted. Homo Erectus, for example, lived for almost 2 million years and thrived in East-Asia. Homo Sapiens conversely, evolved in East-Africa 150,000 years ago, and willingly or unwillingly killed off all the remaining human species. And with our self-destructive tendencies, given the current state of affairs today, we do not even have a good shot at making it to 200,000 years of existence by the look of things.

Beyond that, even amongst our species, there are 7.6 billion humans on the planet today. Ask yourself very honestly, "What makes me more special than any other human being?" Are the rich more special and therefore more deserving of the universe, than the poor because they have accumulated material goods? Does the honest worker deserve more from the universe than the criminal? You may have your opinions, but the simple and unavoidable truth is that the universe does not care, and nature does not play favourites. We all live by the same unbreakable rules of the universe. We all need food, we all need water, we all have a circadian rhythm[3], and we all suffer from the human condition.

---

[3] *Circadian Rhythm is a biological process that displays a repetitive pattern of sleep, digestion, energy levels, etc. over a 24-hour period.*

Any "needs" beyond the universe's imposed rules are superfluous constructs that we, the only remaining human species, have created and we chose to live by them. But this does not change the fact that anything over and above what nature and the universe demands is extra "pretend stuff" that we do not actually need.

Many ancient philosophers manifested this in the way they lived. For example, Diogenes of Sinope who was an eminent philosopher from the school of Cynics had no possessions except for his cloak and staff, and he slept and ate wherever he wanted. In other words, he was homeless by choice. The iconic and famous philosopher was once visited by Alexander the Great, who was an admirer of his teachings. The magnanimous Emperor once visited Diogenes and said that he would grant the philosopher anything he wished for from his vast empire. When Alexander asked Diogenes what he wanted, he replied this: That the Emperor move slightly to his right, as he was blocking the sun.

# 4 VIEW THE WORLD AS IT IS, NOT THE WAY YOU SEE IT

Marcus Aurelius, one of the great Stoic philosophers, was also the Emperor of Rome from 161 A.D. until his death in 180 A.D. During this time, although the Empire prospered and Marcus Aurelius was victorious on the battlefields, his reign was anything but a walk in the park. The Empire was ravaged by floods, multiple devastating earthquakes, and a deadly plague that caused catastrophic damage to the population[4]. On top of the incessant natural disasters, the enemy was fought on all fronts, and so the Emperor-King spent much of his time running his war machine from one side of the Empire to the other. What a tumultuous and tormented reign it must have

---

[4] During his reign, Marcus Aurelius had to manage the *flooding of the Tiber (161), earthquakes at Cyzicus (161) and at Smyrna (178), and the terrible plague epidemic brought back by Roman troops returning from the Parthian war in Asia (166).*

been, yet Marcus Aurelius always seemed calm under pressure, and able to make the fairest and most rational decisions no matter the circumstances. This earned him the moniker of *The Last Good Emperor of Rome*. He made it look easy by all accounts, given the plethora of challenges he and his Empire faced.

His judgment and decision-making was always subject to his three golden rules of thought so he could think clearly. His most famous gift to posterity, *Meditations*, is in fact his own checklists to repeat and follow in order to ensure he remained ultimately objective, good, virtuous, fair and overall a good Stoic. Within these checklists, he included his three golden rules. He would then meditate on these, as in reading and rereading them, which explains how Marcus Aurelius was able to remain the same, even-keeled, fair, wise and capable ruler he was regardless of the circumstances. Condensed and written in plain language, his three golden rules are:

1. Train yourself to fight the Autonomous Loop so as to see the world as it is, not the way you see it.
2. View things in an objective manner by looking at them through other pairs of eyes.
3. Routinely declutter the mind.

The Autonomous Loop is a phenomenon of our efficient brain. The brain is able to quickly identify what information is relevant and what is not (or so it believes) and therefore is able to focus on the task at hand despite sensory overload. For example, the Autonomous Loop is how you can focus on the voice of the person you are conversing with and ignore all other noises in the background even in a very noisy environment. This is efficient, however, efficiency comes with a compromise in quality. If the brain is only registering what it thinks is important, it means you are missing out on a world of information that is right in front of our eyes, literally. At this moment, you are focusing on this sentence and this sentence alone, and therefore are unaware of a whole world around you. Take a moment to look up and view, listen, absorb. The sheer volume of information that is available to you at this moment is immense, yet for a moment there, your brain was solely focused on this text.

"Nothing has such power to broaden the mind as the ability to investigate systematically and truly all that comes under thy observation in life."

- Marcus Aurelius

To make good, rational decisions, take a step back and make sure you have all the information, not just the information you see. Fight the Autonomous Loop whenever you can, and train your mind to view the world the way it is, and not the world your brain's autonomous loop thinks is important (the brain is selfish and riddled with bad coding like this...more on this later).

The second rule is to see things through many pairs of eyes. Your mind is subjective to your reality. And so every other person who has their own reality will see things from a whole other subjective perspective. This is a simple, yet significant point.

Consider this mental exercise: Our subject is an old dog that shows it has had a long and fulfilling life, and that it is on the last leg of its life, standing there with his owner. A dog lover might walk by, and upon seeing the dog pet it and think, "What a cute dog!" Another individual who dislikes dogs might walk by, avoid looking at it all together and think, "What vile creatures they are, with the drooling, shedding and the smell!" A third individual might walk by and upon seeing the dog think, "How sad, the poor thing looks like it will die soon." Yet another person might walk by, and upon seeing the dog think, "What a lucky dog, as it looks like it has lived a long and fulfilling happy life, and will live out the rest of his days with its owner in a loving home." Its owner might be looking at the dog thinking, "I wonder if the dog is in the mood to go to the park and play fetch?" And finally, this whole time, the dog may be thinking, "Maybe that human has a treat for me! Or maybe that one!" Here are six realities and narratives about the same subject. Yet they are all very different from one another, as each of their perspectives are dependent on, and shaped by their senses, mental models, past experiences, fear, wishes and wants. The lesson here is that by viewing the problem, issue, or event through other pairs of eyes, you can harness an objective view, or at least get closer to it than merely looking at it from your own perspective, which is biased.

Finally, Marcus Aurelius emphasizes decluttering the mind often and on a regular basis. The brain is a noisy place. In your brain, at any given moment, you are not only thinking about the task at hand. However, floating around in there you also have your feelings, thoughts, questions, memories, to-do lists, grocery lists, worries, etc. There is so much happening in there that often you do not recognize all that goes through your mind as they get lost in the hustle and bustle of your churning brain. A thought or an idea you had might later be forgotten. A negative thought, event or issue to be dealt with might never be addressed and float around your mind in the background becoming a proverbial thorn on your side without being rationalized, then fester up and cause angst. And so to avoid such situations, we must declutter the mind. Grab a pen and some paper and put your thoughts on paper. Keep a journal. When your ideas are on paper, they not only present themselves in a different light, but they also come out to the forefront to be rationally dealt with. When a thought, idea or decision is rationally broken down and examined on paper, you essentially have a rational conversation with yourself and approach the problem with your rational ordinary mind (ordinary mind meaning a mind without emotions). Declutter the mind by writing once, or several times a day.

"Nobody can give you wiser advice than yourself."
- Marcus Tullius Cicero

# 5 LIFE IS A SHORT-TERM PHENOMENON

The Apollo space program, a technological marvel by any measure, brought man to the moon. The towering rockets sent daredevil maverick test pilots turned astronauts from earth to another celestial object in space. It was the pinnacle of human technological achievement in its time and still is the furthest humans have traveled in space. It was, and still is the only feat of its kind.

On July 20, 1969, Neil Armstrong took the first step on the moon, thus meeting the challenge laid down by John F. Kennedy back in 1961 to send astronauts to the moon and back before the end of the decade.[5] When the astronauts came

---

[5] *On September 12, 1962, in his famous "We choose to go to the Moon speech," President John F. Kennedy addressed a large crowd at the Rice Stadium in Houston, Texas, and laid down the challenge to the nation of landing an American on the Moon and safely returning them to earth before the end of the decade.*

back from the moon missions, they became instant celebrities. The first man to step on the moon, of course, was in a celebrity class of his own, and his quote from his first step is etched in the annals of time:

"That's one small step for man, one giant leap for mankind."

- Neil Armstrong

Yet even in his newfound worldwide fame, Neil Armstrong and his wife went back to live on their farm in Maryland, just as they lived before the Apollo program. This was surprising for most, but not for the former editor of *Aviation Week Magazine* and a longtime friend of Armstrong:

"You get out on the farm. You look at the mountains across the valley, which are several million years old and are going to be there through the life of the planet. You understand that you're a short-term phenomenon, like the mosquitos that come in the spring and fall. You get a perspective on yourself. You're getting back to the fundamentals of the planet."

- Robert Hotz

Life indeed is fleeting, ephemeral, short and impermanent.

---

*Between July 20, 1969, (first landing) and December 14, 1972, (last lunar liftoff), six separate Apollo missions landed 12 astronauts on the surface of the moon and safely returned all of them.*

In his essay *On Transience*, Sigmund Freud sites a conversation he had with the young poet Rilke. As they were walking through this beautiful park full of life, blooming flowers and chirping birds Rilke suddenly and visibly got teary-eyed. When Freud questioned his friend as to how he could be so melancholy while being surrounded by all this beauty. Rilke responded that he was sad because he realized that all this beauty, these trees, colourful flowers, the cheerful birds, all of this were one day going to die. Death is unavoidable, inescapable and inevitable.

> "Man is literally split in two: he has an awareness of his own splendid uniqueness in that he sticks out of nature with a towering majesty, and yet he goes back into the ground a few feet in order blindly and dumbly to rot and disappear forever."
>
> - Ernest Becker

In the cosmic scale of things, you already know that you will be around, at best, for 0.00000000725% of the known life of the universe. But, even amongst our species' timeline, we will only be around for a minuscule portion of it. The Genus *Homo* evolved around 2 million years ago, so of all the human species' timeline, you will be around at best for 0.00005%.

Life, your life, is a short-term phenomenon. Take a moment to think how much of your life has gone by already. Now think about how much you have left. Close your eyes and ask yourself "How much is left before eternal darkness and nothingness?"

If this hasn't caused some minor anxiety in you, then you have not fully embraced how fleeting life is and how precious little of it you have left. If that is the case, go back and reread the last paragraph until it does. Conversely, if you did get some anxiety from this, then you are finally ready to begin *living* your life as opposed to just being alive.

To truly recognize the fragility of your time here is humbling. Now use that perspective to identify what is truly important, and what is unimportant. With this perspective, take a moment to think of a few unimportant, or trivial matters you used to stress over, that really does not merit any of your precious time being wasted on after realizing how very little of it you actually have. A small mental exercise you can do is to imagine you knew for sure you were going to die at the end of the month. How many things you currently worry about just became unimportant in this scenario? So why would changing this expiration date to 1 year, 10 years or 100 years change what is important?

Do not fear death. The anxiety that came with the sudden realization of the shortness of the remainder of your life is not from the prospect of death. The anxiety is from not knowing whether you are making the most of your time while you are here. Are you missing out? Are you wasting your precious time? These are uncertainties, and only uncertain things cause anxiety. Death is a sure thing. It is simply a matter of time, not if. To fear something that is assured to happen is ludicrous and a self-inflicted punishment. You will die. This will happen. You have no choice over this as death is a universal law for all life. What you can do however is use that knowledge of death and impermanence to better live your life today. Do not fear death, quite the opposite remember that you are dying every day, so as to motivate you to live a full life while you have it. The Stoics lived by this mantra and embodied it in two words: *Memento Mori*. Remember death. Remember impermanence. Reminding yourself of this inescapable and unavoidable truth regularly will help you immediately see what is important and truly merits your time, and what is trivial and does not deserve to tax your precious time.

Research shows that mammals have an average set number of heartbeats for their lifetimes. Giraffes average about 680 million heartbeats in their lifetime, rabbits about 970 million, monkeys about 1.5 billion, and us humans get about 2.2 billion. For humans, however, with the advent of modern medicine, we can push the general estimate to about 3 billion. Stop for a moment, close your eyes, and listen to your heart beating. Each beat brings you closer to the end. *Tick tock*. Never forget this and let this motivate you to live a better life today and for the rest of your days.

The day you die is not death. Every day is death. Every day is another day gone by that you will not get back. The day you die is simply the last death. But every day is death. The past is gone. You can learn from it, but there is no option to change any of it. The future holds a script for you, which you do not yet know and cannot know, control or change. So do not live in the memories of the past or the hopes of the future. You are dying right now, this is a fact. And so live as if you are dying right now. Use this freeing reality to unburden yourself from the trivial matters in life that you used to worry about. See things in a proper perspective (what truly is important and what is not) and live every day, as opposed to living in memories and hopes. Live right now.

"Life is very short and anxious for those who forget the past, neglect the present, and fear the future."

- Lucius Annaeus Seneca

# 6 ACTORS AND SPECTATORS

All matter is energy, and if matter were to accelerate to a velocity of 299,792,458 meters per second (the speed of light), it would then turn into pure, massless energy. Albert Einstein famously summarized this theory in his iconic equation $E=mc^2$. Although he will be etched in history for his work on the Theory of Relativity, he has many other less known contributions to posterity. For example, he was also very outspoken about his religious beliefs.

> "Science without religion is lame, religion without science is blind."
>
> - Albert Einstein

Albert Einstein was a pantheist[6]. He believed in Spinoza's god. The universe was his god, and for good reason, as he believed in determinism due to its simple logic. Try this mental exercise to understand the deduction supporting determinism.

If you were to drop a ball on the floor, with certain measurements at hand (height and weight of the ball, the elasticity of both surfaces, etc.), noting the forces at play, mainly the force of gravity at 9.81 meters per second squared, you can use Newtonian equations to calculate how high the ball will bounce. You know from high school math and science that equipped with the pertinent equation, any outcome can be predicted and calculated as long as you have all the variables you would require to make said calculation. The more variables are available to us to plug in our equations, the more predictions one can make of varying events.

At a certain point, however, the human brain simply cannot calculate all the variables for a complex prediction, such as two galaxies colliding, and the ensuing outcome of said collision. Enter computer simulations. We have simulations that show what will happen when Andromeda collides with our galaxy, the Milky Way, in about 4 billion years. Therefore with known equations and known quantified variables, using computer

---

[6] *Albert Einstein believed in Baruch Spinoza's god, which is the universe and its laws and guiding forces that have created the marvelous order in which it all works. He stated that believing in a personal god who cares about the individual is naive and egocentric.*

simulators one could predict a whole lot more than you can with just our human brains.

However, even computers have their limitations. Add to that the fact that we do not yet have equations for many phenomena, and could not possibly amass all the variables that happen around us due to their sheer quantity. But if we were to consider a hypothetical scenario, where the computer had limitless computational power, and the computer had on record, all the events that ever occurred everywhere from the beginning of the Big Bang to date, then it could accurately calculate and predict everything that was about to happen in the next second, then the next, then the next.

This is true for even your behaviour and decisions. You would like to think that you have free will and your experiences and mental models are unique. After all, your decisions are based on your knowledge, your feelings, your mood, your environment, the given context of a decision. Therefore the decision you make must be unique to you and only you, right? After all, you are the only one who knows and feels all this. Well, with that in mind think of another hypothetical scenario, where one could create a perfect simulation of you in a machine, with all the information of your past, all your feelings, knowledge, and all the variables of the environment, the context of the decision, etc. If it was a perfect replica of you internally, you externally and of your environment, it could very accurately predict how you will behave, act and make decisions. It would be able to predict your decisions and actions, as it would be basing its decisions and actions on all of the same variables you are basing yours on. It would have the same belief of free will, the same chemical composition dictating its whims, and same database of knowledge, memories, and self-image.

Such a machine, of course, never could exist. To replicate all those variables is impossible due to the sheer quantity of information. Today, we have only one machine – the universe itself – that is big enough and powerful enough to compute the outcome of what will happen now. It contains within it all the past information and variables. And therefore a machine to predict the future before it happens would necessarily have to be bigger than the universe. And so our capacity to accurately predict the future is limited to smaller isolated problems. We can accurately predict the position of Mars a hundred years from now, as the information (variables) required are manageable and the necessary equations to solve the problem (predict its future location) are known to us. However, due to the sheer number of variables and lack of predictive equations of human behaviour, we cannot possibly build a simulator to predict your behaviour. This is a fact.

However, the point of this mental exercise was not to believe that we can predict the future of everything, including your behaviour. It was to see the logic that theoretically, "reality" can be duplicated in a simulation to identically imitate "reality" in what happens next. This is possible as reality is based on a series of prior events. Remind yourself that when you make a decision using your "free will," you are making the decision "freely" based on your mood, wishes, wants, likes, fears, past knowledge, current physical state, current external state, etc. In other words, you make it based on a series of variables. And if 100% of all variables that affect your decision can be put into a simulator machine, the machine would make the same decisions as you will.

> "Whatever happens to you has been waiting to happen since the beginning of time. The twining strands of fate wove both of them together."
>
> - Marcus Aurelius

Those variables that drive your current decision, make your current decision predetermined. In turn, the variables you base your decisions on were outcome events based on other variables that came before them. And those were based on variables that came before them, and so forth, going all the way back to the first thing (that we know of), the Big Bang. Therefore, one can conclude that everything that happened in the past, is happening now and will happen in the future can be traced back through a sequence of events (causes and consequences) dating back 13.8 billion years to the Big Bang.

> "Everyone who is seriously involved in the pursuit of science becomes convinced that a spirit is manifest in the laws of the Universe, a spirit vastly superior to that of man, and one in the face of which we with our modest powers must feel humble. My religion consists of a humble admiration of the illimitable superior spirit

who reveals himself in the slight details we are able to perceive with our frail and feeble mind."

- Albert Einstein

The thought that everything is predetermined and predestined is a chilling idea indeed. This would make you merely an actor of what the universe has scripted for you. However, as human beings, we do not have the capacity to "remember" the future. In our dimension time flows only in one direction: From past to future. And so we truly do not know what lies ahead for us in the future. This then makes us spectators of the same script. You are both an actor of the cosmic script that intertwines everything in the known universe and a spectator.

Determinism does not state that you have no choices in life. It simply outlines the logic that all events past, present and future, can be tied together via causes and consequences. Even though all that will be and all that you do is predetermined, the illusion of free will is all too real, as we have neither a copy of the script nor a machine that could read it if we did. So you must live your life as if you have free will and make choices. Good choices.

# 7 QUE SERA SERA

"If you are annoyed at something, it is because you have forgotten:

1. That everything happens in accordance with universal nature;
2. That whatever fault was committed is not your concern; and
3. Moreover, that everything that happens has always happened thus, and will always happen thus, and is, at this very moment, happening thus everywhere."

- Marcus Aurelius

As you make the best choices you can, remind yourself that the universe already holds the script that dictates all that is to come. Not just for you but for all matter in the universe. The universe does not owe you anything. The universe will do what it will, regardless of your hopes and wishes. Therefore, reason would dictate that you should not hope for things to be a certain way, as the outcome is out of your control. And since you are at the mercy of what fate will dish out at you, by hoping for a certain outcome you are negatively labeling any other outcome other than the one you wish for. And so more often than not you would be faced with a perceived negative outcome when in reality it is not. It just *is*.

Along with *Memento Mori*, the Stoics lived by *Amor Fati*: Love fate. Whatever happens, happens. Whatever happened, happened – and you have no recourse, no options to change that, no other reality to go to where it happened differently. Regardless of how positive or negative an event, it happened and it is in the past. Now it is up to your judgment, and only your judgment of said past event to determine if it was "good" or "bad," and ultimately how you react to it.

All these concepts good, bad, fair or unfair are a construct of your own imagination. Three billion heartbeats. *Tick tock*. Did getting cut off in traffic really merit an emotional response, or worse a physical manifestation of that emotional response? Did your blood pressure rise? Did your heart rate speed up? Was that really necessary or important? Never forget 3 billion heartbeats and every day is death. *Tick tock*.

And thus you can easily remark that many of your afflicted feelings are in fact frivolous, irrelevant and unimportant. They are trivial. They are meaningless in the grand scheme of things. You, with your rational ordinary mind, can see that these trivial matters merit no worry and that drawing anxiety from them is wasteful of your time, your own doing, ludicrous and self-harming. But what of the emotions you feel that make you angry and act out? What of the emotions you cannot control? What of them? I ask you, do you truly believe you are at the mercy of your emotions? Emotions are simply bad coding in your brain. Pre-registered response packages based on memories of past events. More on this bad coding later, but for now it would suffice to recognize that emotions are simply bad coding in that they are pre-registered responses to events. Your rational ordinary mind does not want them, especially the negative ones, as it knows they are internal to you, your own doing and counterproductive to your state of mind.

The Stoics recognized this as well and rejected emotions. This practice is embodied in the mantra *Amor Fati* and rejected all the good and bad things fate threw their way. Fate is not you. You are you. External factors do not determine how you feel at any given moment. You do. Your judgment of the event does. You have the controls, so use that control instead of giving into the bad coding.

Buddha said life is flux. What will happen will happen. You must go with the flow, as there simply is no other alternative. To wish and hope for something different, something better is ludicrous as it is impossible to change what is. The universe is flux, and you must flow with these changes, good or bad, like a leaf falling from a branch, not knowing which way it will fly or ultimately where it will land.

Buddha also encouraged meditating on feelings. All feelings, good or bad. The key to nirvana is to understand and embrace that feelings are fleeting. All feelings come and go. There is no possible state in which one can be happy, angry, sad or elated at all times. Feelings come and necessarily always go, like water floating around pillars of a bridge, and therefore we should not pay any mind to emotions. They have no materiality, or impact on us that remains within us. They pass. Be like the pillar, and let the emotions go as they come. The day you can ignore all emotions without it affecting you or changing your behaviour or thoughts in any way is the day you have reached nirvana, a peace infinitely more gratifying than happiness.

You get upset when things do not go your way. So just go the way things are, then everything is your way.

# 8 THERE IS NO FAIR OR UNFAIR

There is neither fair nor unfair. You are owed nothing. Your life is an infinitesimally small part of the vast universe, so to think you are owed a favourable outcome because you deserve it is ignorant and egocentric. What's more, considering an alternative reality where the results of events are more favourable for you is ludicrous and harmful to one's self. "If only I had got that job" or "If only this had happened or that happened" are self-inflicted wounds. There is no *if.* There only *is*, and you quite literally have no choice in the matter, so why bother to wish and hope of another sci-fi, hypothetical, nonexistent alternative universe where things would have been different?

The universe did what it did. There is no altering reality, there is no going back and there is no real option to change what happened. So why would you waste any time thinking of this alternative reality, or worse, make yourself upset over it? Time is fleeting. Three billion heartbeats. *Tick tock*. Do you want to spend the next 100 or 500 or 1000 heartbeats in angst due to your own imagination running amok? Angst that is caused 100% by your own doing, by thinking of an alternative reality where things were more "fair" for you, that can never be?

In the collections *Letter from a Stoic*, Seneca tells his friend Lucilious about a harsh yet true consolation letter he sent to another friend of his, Marcia. Marcia was the daughter of the prominent historian Aulus Cremutius Cordus. Marcia had lost her son Metilius, and her suffering became chronic where she was still grieving after three years. He reminds her about her father's death, who she loved just as dearly as her son, and how she was at peace with his death after adequately mourning for a while. He pointed out that fate gives and takes life without question, and asked her who are we to think one death is worse than the other. He tells her that children die all the time, and for her to grieve so much is due to her illusion that her child did not deserve to die as he is more special than other children. Furthermore, there is no other reality where he might still be alive. There is simply this reality and life is thus; it is as it is. He says it is normal to grieve after a death, as is the case with all deaths. However, to hold on to grief so long because it was a death of a child and not an elderly person is her own doing and for no good reason.

"What madness this is, to punish oneself because one is unfortunate, and not to lessen, but to increase one's ills! ... For there is such a thing as self-restraint in grief also."

- Lucius Annaeus Seneca

*Memento Mori*: Remember Death. Death, like birth and change, is in conformity with the universe. Therefore, to fear or try to reject something that is 1) In conformity with the universe, and 2) Absolutely inevitable is ludicrous and self-inflicted.

Too often you see what is good as normal, and what is normal as bad. Take a moment to think about your situation. No matter how bad it is, there is always a way for it to get worse. Do you have your vision? Think about a scenario where you would be blind. Think about the difficulties of navigating your day to day life. Do you have both your arms? Imagine a scenario where you are missing one, or both your arms. Think about the challenges of having to get through your days limbless. Do you have loved ones? Think about a scenario where one, some or all have passed tragically early. Go hungry for a day or two and imagine not having anything to eat for days on end on a regular basis. When you are sad over your situation and think "Why me?" or "So unfair" remind yourself that it is not the situation that is bad, as your situation is good compared to a worse situation. You see the situation as being bad simply because of your bad judgment of the situation. See the situation objectively instead and see that regardless of its challenges, it is still a good situation compared to other worse ones.

> "Do not spoil what you have by desiring what you have not; remember that what you now have was once among the things you only hoped for."
>
> - Epicurus

The point is no matter what ails you, there is always a way for things to be worse. And this is what you have to meditate on, as it is the only way you will not take your current situation for granted.

And when your situation is good, remember, the universe did not provide you with this good fortune because it owes it to you. Your reality is the way it is, period. And so your situation is good, only because you judge it to be as such.

Do not imagine a scenario where things are better for you. This is false, as that is a scenario that is not your current reality. Right now you are here, as the way things are, and nothing can change that. So go the way things are and appreciate it. You do not need fate to give you good or bad things to manage your state of mind. Your judgment of events, good or bad sets your mood.

> "Man is affected, not by events, but by the views he takes of them."
>
> - Epictetus

Our sensory nerves are fast. Very fast. They speed information of our surroundings to our brains in microseconds. However, as you form your judgment and response to an external event, remind yourself that the event, albeit by microseconds, is already in the past. Whatever you are judging or responding to is inevitably always in the past, as we cannot observe something before it happens. Therefore, meditate on this and remind yourself that any and all judgments and responses, you and you alone chose to make. Your rational ordinary mind does not want to respond in a prepackaged manner because something happened. *Said* event is in the past. To use a past event as an excuse to behave one way or another is a false justification for your future actions. You are you, everything else in the universe is external to you, and your rational ordinary mind wants to always be the *good you* regardless of what happens around you. Go the way things are as opposed to getting upset over them. There is only the here and now. *Amor Fati.*

"It is not what happens to you, but how you react to it that matters."

- Epictetus

No event, no person, no words or nothing fate delivers deserves you to break good judgment and waste precious time being afflicted. If you do, it is literally your choice to do so. Three billion heartbeats. *Tick tock.* How do you want to spend yours? In self-inflicted negative emotions, or going the way things go? Three billion heartbeats. *Tick tock.*

But this is easier said than done right? When you are calm and use your rational ordinary mind you agree with all this as it makes sense. But when emotions hit you, you simply cannot control yourself. Or rather, it is very difficult to control yourself. However, you must. Your rational ordinary mind does not want to keep living this Dr. Jekyll and Mr. Hyde scenario. And so meditate on your rational ordinary mind.

Meditate on the bridge, with its pillars standing firm in the water, while the water rushes past. Your rational ordinary mind is the bridge with the pillars, and your emotions are the water. See them, recognize them and accept that they are there and may change your mood. A pocket of cold water will temporarily change the temperature of the pillars. However. this pocket of cold water will pass, and the pillars will return normal temperature. In the same way, emotions will pass and your mood will return to normal. The important thing here is that your state of mind will not change. You will remain tranquil and your rational ordinary mind will remain firm in place, like the bridge and its pillars that remain solid, as emotions and moods come and go.

Write this down. Read it. Rewrite it and reread it. Sit in solitude, close your eyes, and think of it. Visualise the bridge and the flowing water. Through repetition and time, you will find more and more that emotions will be there without changing your physical or mental composition in any way. You will be able to remain you, the true you, with your rational ordinary mind regardless of circumstances.

# 9 BAD CODING

Why do you find it so hard not to feel and act on emotions, when your rational ordinary mind, whilst calm, logically understands that you should not be afflicted by emotional responses or reactions? They are, after all, a waste of energy, and more importantly of your precious time. It is due to bad coding? Emotional responses are like bad coding in that through nature and, mostly, nurture, your brain has adopted a series of IF-THEN-THEREFORE statements that are prepackaged automated responses to events in your environment.

For example, you see someone illegally cut in traffic ahead of you. This not only breaks the social contract, but it causes you to miss the green light by one car, which you otherwise would have made (IF "jerk driver does bad"). Due to feelings of being unfairly mistreated and unjustly delayed on your way home after a long day of work, chemicals associated with that feeling get triggered in the body (THEN "perceive situation as being unfair thus releasing Epinephrine into bloodstream"), and you turn into the Incredible Hulk as you lash out a few choice words and flip the designated finger (THEREFORE "lose your $&*T").

> "Does the event which has happened to you prevent you from being just, from possessing greatness of soul, from being temperant and prudent, without haste in your judgments, without falsity in your speech, reserved, and free, and everything else such that, when they are present together, the nature of man possesses that which is proper to it?"
>
> - Epictetus

Your rational ordinary mind knows life just *is*, and that the universe just *is*, and that there is no other reality where things could have gone differently. It knows to simply accept what *is* with tranquility as any other response is a waste of time, precious time, and a self-inflicted punishment. Therefore every emotion – happiness, sadness, aroused, angered, jealous, bitter, elated, fear, disgust, etc. – is essentially a pre-established IF-THEN-THEREFORE statement that does not conform with your rational ordinary mind. Our Western culture simply does not teach the more appropriate responses from an early age, and we end up adopting responses we see around us, from our elders, television, movies and stories.

In July 2018, a dozen kids at the young and tender age of 13-14 became trapped in underground caves in Thailand following a flashflood during their hike of the caves. No escape, only a narrow exit now flooded under an immense quantity of subterranean waters, literally buried alive. It took rescuers more than two weeks to get them out. Think about being stuck underground with no means of escape, in your own dark tomb, for more than two weeks, and at such a tender age no less. Just the mental image is eerily terrifying and a justifiable cause of anxiety. The thought of this situation is easily more than enough to invoke anxiety in you and most other Westerners. Yet as news emerged from the cave, the public saw pictures of tranquil meditating kids who were at peace and waiting patiently and bravely for rescue. Again, think about how you would have reacted. Most probably by manifesting an unwanted emotion like fear or anger or panic. Not these kids, they did not have the same bad coding you have.

Daniel Kahneman wrote a book entirely on the topic of knee-jerk response versus the rational ordinary response of a nobler kind. He referred to the inherent "autopilot" responses as System One, and the more thought out and logical responses as System Two. Freud referred to these as the Id and the Ego, whereby the Id controls your intuitive instinctive reaction, and the Ego dictates your more controlled and thought out responses. Many have studied and discussed the topic of the Lizard brain versus the Mammal brain, and these studies go far beyond simply responses to events. For the purposes of your reflections, however, simply understand that there is a discourse within you. There is the part of you that is rational and responds clearly, virtuously and compassionately. Then there is the side of you that is emotional and badly coded. Not badly coded in that you have emotions, as emotions are a part of being human and unavoidable. But badly coded in that you instinctively respond based on emotions and said response may be contrary to what your rational ordinary mind would have done.

> "The intuitive mind is a sacred gift and the rational mind is a faithful servant. We have created a society that honours the servant and has forgotten the gift."
>
> - Albert Einstein

This bad coding in you can be changed. Through practice you can correct your intuitive mind to act in a way that is in conformity with your rational ordinary mind. Through practice, by reminding yourself of everything you have read, and everything you will read here, through their application and repetition the bad coding can slowly be changed. But you have to start somewhere. Remind yourself you spent years learning, going to school and absorbing information in your day to day life in order to feed and train your rational mind. You must also spend some time feeding and training your intuitive mind.

A good starting point is realizing events are not excuses to act in a base way. They are not an excuse to let out any harbouring negative feelings you have towards the world. Everything that happens is already in the past and therefore should not have any bearing on your responses or actions in the present. A good perspective is a foundation for all Stoic behaviour, which is that only moral good or virtue, is good; and only moral evil or vice is an evil.

> "On the occasion of everything that causes you sadness, remember to use this 'dogma': not only is this not a misfortune, but it is a piece of good fortune for you to bear up under it courageously."
>
> - Marcus Aurelius

This must mean that what happens external to your thoughts and mind should have no bearing whatsoever on your state of mind. Said otherwise, the choice of your state of mind, of which you clearly want tranquility as opposed to anxiety, is quite literally and entirely up to you in how you respond to the external events. Epictetus was known to tell his auditors that eliminating all "Alas!" and "How unhappy I am!" from one's life is critical.

Repeat the good dogma. Write it down. Read it. Do this multiple times a day and for the rest of your life. The pursuit of tranquility is a lifelong journey, and each repetition of your dogmas, creed or mantra (whatever you want to call it) is a step towards the end of this path. Each time you face, what could have otherwise been an unwelcome event, with a newfound embrace of it simply being what the universe has in store, and that it is immaterial to your state of mind, and to just go with it, you take another step down this path. Step by step you must try and become a philosopher king.

# 10 WHO AM I?

Do the following mental exercise: Theseus, the mythical king and founder-hero of Athens, had a ship. The Ship of Theseus was known far and wide for its use in battle by the great hero. When Theseus passed away, the townspeople decided to maintain the ship. And so one day when a plank was seen to be old, aged and warped, it was replaced. The new plank emulated the old one exactly in every way, but the ship no longer had all its original parts as used in battle by Theseus. Is it still the Ship of Theseus?

Time goes by and now a few dozen planks and ropes have been replaced. Is it still the Ship of Theseus?

More time goes by, now most of the old planks and ropes have been replaced, along with a sail. Is it still the Ship of Theseus?

Eventually, all of the original parts of the ship get replaced. Recall that each plank and rope and sail was perfectly replicated and replaced in the exact same way as the original ship, so as to maintain the pristine ship. At this point still, is it the Ship of Theseus?

Now imagine that someone had been gathering the old pieces, as they were being removed, and reassembled the entire ship on land (as it cannot possibly float with its aged and warped lumber). However, this ship assembled on land not only has the pieces assembled in the original way but actually has the original parts. Is this the Ship of Theseus? Is it the other new one in the harbor that perfectly replicates the original one but also floats? Are there two Ships of Theseus? Or none?

So who are you? As you age from infancy and grow, then grow old and shrink, your body changes. Which body are you? If you get a pacemaker, have laser eye surgery, or have an ear implant to hear better, are you still you? If you lose both your legs in a car accident and your legs are amputated, are you half you?

These questions inevitably point to the undeniable truth that you, the real "you," must necessarily be independent of your body, as no matter what happens to your body you are still you. Therefore you must be the only thing that remains independent of your physical body, yet is still part of it, or rather within it: your thoughts and your consciousness. You are what lives inside your brain, that sees the world from within.

This is an important distinction, given that if your body is independent from you, then no matter what is happening to your body the real you can still be tranquil. This is how the Dalai Lama remains tranquil when he is violently ill. The pain and illness shall pass, but he will not use this external factor to harness sadness and anxiety, as this would be his own doing. And why would he willingly make an uncomfortable situation (physical discomfort from being ill) worse by also making his mind ill.

"How does it help…to make troubles heavier by bemoaning them?"

- Lucius Annaeus Seneca

In a similar fashion, the Stoic who is being tortured will remain tranquil. Even though his body is in pain, as the pain of the torture does not prevent him from remaining virtuous and rational. His body may be in pain, but the real him, his rational ordinary mind remains untouched and therefore remains rational and virtuous.

"Nevertheless there have been men who have not uttered a moan amid these tortures. 'More yet!' says the torturer; but the victim has not begged for release. 'More yet!' he says again; but no answer has come. 'More yet!' the victim has smiled, and heartily, too. Can you not bring yourself, after an example like this, to make a mock at pain?"

- Lucius Annaeus Seneca

Your body is an external factor to the real you. And no external factor should affect you, as it is not part of you. Once again, it is your judgment of the event, not the event itself, that determines how you act and react. And your judgment, as your rational ordinary mind knows, should remain rational. If you react negatively, or in anger, your *eye for an eye* mentality is your own doing. It is not someone else's fault, nor does the universe owe you a reality where you are not in pain and suffering. *Amor Fati*, go with the way things are.

> "It follows that the only evil or trouble there can be for us resides in our own judgment; that is to say, in the way we represent things to ourselves; and that people are the authors of their own problems. Everything, therefore, is a matter of judgment. The intellect is independent of the body, and things do not come inside us in order to trouble us. If everything is a matter of judgment, every fault is, in fact, a false judgment and proceeds from ignorance."
>
> - Marcus Aurelius

You ask yourself, but if someone or fate itself is doing something bad to me, do I not have the right to be upset? Do you? Should any event justify you not being what your rational ordinary mind wants to be: Tranquil? And what is good? What is bad? Can an event be bad? Only if we consider an alternative reality in which said event never occurred. This you know is not an option, there is only the current reality. Therefore the event is not a bad event, it just *is*. And the same goes for a good event. When fate brings you something good, you should not be ecstatic, or elated, or proud. The event is not a good event, it just *is*, and therefore should not change you and the way you want to be: Tranquil.

The Stoic therefore knows external events cannot be good or bad any more than they can be fair or unfair. Therefore good and bad can only be derived from things that are dependent on you and under your control. And what is under your control? Only your thoughts. Your judgments, choices and your assent to the will of the universe depends on you. Everything else depends on the universe and fate.

# 11 LOVE THY NEIGHBOUR

"Only the development of compassion and understanding for others can bring us the tranquility and happiness we all seek."

- Dalai Lama

If you have accepted that all events are external and that the only thing you control is your judgment of and choice of response to *said* events, and that your rational ordinary mind wants to be virtuous and tranquil, then you also understand that no matter how degenerately someone is acting towards you, it does not stop you from responding with kindness and compassion in return.

Some people are toxic, and you may not want them around you, in which case you simply walk away and don't keep toxic people around you. However, in the likely scenario where you will at times be confronted by one, any angry or disgraceful response or action on your part is your own choosing. An eye for an eye is an excuse to act in a negative, angry, violent and vengeful way. Whatever is done to you, it is already in the past. There is no fair, or unfair, there is no good or bad event. There is only your good/bad judgment and your virtue/disgracefulness. Three billion heartbeats. *Tick tock*. How do you want to react? Which response do you think will harbour tranquility?

The Dalai Lama himself said sometimes a situation requires a stern response. However, there is always a way to be kind and compassionate even in said stern response. And the Stoic will say that no situation, a person's actions or anything external to you for that matter has an impact on your actions or holds sway over your virtue. You control your judgments, and so if you chose to judge something or someone as being bad, you are making a false value judgment.

If your judgment still believes someone wronged you, remind yourself that this was a mistake on their part due to one of three reasons:

1. They were not objectively seeing the world as it is and were seeing it only through their eyes, and therefore did not even realize they were wronging you.
2. You, knowingly or unknowingly, wronged them. They in return sought vengeance (an eye for an eye) as they do not know any better.

3. They are the type of being who derives joy from the misery of others and wronged you on purpose, once again for a lack of not knowing any better.

You, however, know better. You know that all wrongdoing comes from disorder and irrationality. You are neither of those. You have a rational ordinary mind. Therefore, someone knowingly or unknowingly wronging you does not have any bearing on how you act or react and certainly does not give justification in the least on reacting in a negative or disgraceful way. You are not in the pursuit of a life where your goal is to inflict as much pain into the world as it did on to you. You are not in the pursuit of a life of *an eye for an eye* or a life of revenge or anger. Three billion heartbeats. *Tick tock.* No, you are in the pursuit of a tranquil life. Your virtues and rational judgment would never want to hurt any other sentient being, as this will inevitably come with its own guilt and anxieties. The best way to get even with degenerate people is not to resemble them.

Unfortunately, in our competition-driven society, human beings tend to think selfishly. However, the Dalai Lama never inconveniences another sentient being for his own convenience. To prove the point about selflessness and love of everyone, not just one's selves, the Dalai Lama offers a mental exercise involving you and a group of people who are destitute:

1. Notice your natural experience of "I," as in "I want this," "I do not want that."

2. Recognize that it is natural to want happiness and to not want pain. This is valid and does not require further justification.

3. Based on this natural desire, you have the right to obtain happiness and to get rid of suffering.

4. Just as you have this right, so do others, and in equal measure.

5. Consider the fact that the difference between yourself and others is only that you are just one single person, whereas there are countless other living beings on this planet alone.

6. Ask yourself 'Should I use every living being to attain my happiness, or should I help others gain happiness?'

7. Imagine yourself, calm and reasonable, looking to your right at another version of yourself – but this self is overly proud, never thinking of the welfare of others, concerned only with his or her own self.

8. On your left visualize a number of destitute people unrelated to you, needy and in pain.

9. You, in the middle, are an unbiased, sensible person. Consider that those people on both sides of you want happiness and want to get rid of pain; in this way, they are equal, the same.

10. But think this selfishly motivated person on the right is just one person, whereas the others are far greater in number. Which side is more important, the one with the single, self-centered person, or the vast group of poor, helpless people? As the unbiased person in the

middle, you will naturally favour the greater number of suffering people.

11. Reflect on this thought: If I as one person take advantage of the many, it would be truly contrary to my humanity, and to common sense. To sacrifice a lot for the sake of a little is foolish.

12. Thinking this way, you will decide: I am going to direct my energies to the many rather than the selfish person.

Through his Theory of Relativity, Einstein showed that Space and Time are interwoven, forming the fabric of spacetime. If you are a tiny fraction of time ($7.25 \times 10^{-9}\%$), how does our space, our planet Earth, fare in the cosmic scale of things? It is about $3.08 \times 10^{-58}\%$ of the known universe. Note that this number, if written out, would have 57 decimal points written down before the 308%. Therefore your space – the planet – is even smaller than your point in time. The crosspoint between these two infinitesimally small numbers makes for a lot of zeroes.

In the cosmic scale of things, the odds of you being in this point of spacetime, with the people around you, is so incredibly small, it is almost an impossibility. The astronomical odds of you being here, at this point in time and on this planet with the 7.6 billion human beings is so extremely unlikely, you must see others as being fellow passengers, brothers, sisters that are sharing the same improbable odds as you. To share something so unique and so rare and improbable is a bond you cannot ignore and must never forget.

# 12 SERIOUSLY, LOVE THY NEIGHBOUR AND STOP THE DIVISIVENESS

On August 6, 1945, the first atomic bomb used in combat was dropped by the United States on Hiroshima killing an estimated 90,000 to 145,000 Japanese, most of which were civilians. On August 9, 1945, President Harry S. Truman ordered the dropping of the second atomic bomb on Nagasaki, killing another 40,000-80,000 Japanese, who were also mostly civilians. President Harry S. Truman is the only world leader in history to order the use of such a devastating weapon in combat against an enemy (and sadly, most casualties were civilians). The damage and residual radiation have cause devastation, mutations, sickness and death. By any measure, the two atomic bombs were the worst, most destructive weapons ever used in human history. President Harry S. Truman, the man who ordered the dropping of the single most destructive bombs in human history on Japanese civilians, given the circumstances, made the right decision.

Throughout the course of World War II, the Allies continuously bombed Nazi-occupied Europe, strategically targeting key facilities of the war machine. However, the Allies knew that at some point they would have to inevitably put soldiers, tanks, and artillery on the ground to defeat Adolf Hitler's Nazi Germany. On June 6, 1944, the Allied troops landed on the beaches of Normandy. D-Day was the beginning of the end for Adolf Hitler and his Nazis. The Allies from the landing site on the West, and Stalin's Red Army from the border with Russia on the East, slowly descended on Berlin. On May 1, 1945, the Nazis were defeated, and the Americans then turned their undivided attention to the war in the Pacific with the Japanese Empire, which was still ongoing.

The strategy in the Pacific was the same as it was in Europe: Bomb runs with long-range bombers to cripple the war machine, then land forces near and on the main island to finish off the Empire. The first landing operation was codenamed operation Olympic and was scheduled for November 1, 1945. The Japanese knew the Americans would try landing on the main island and march on Tokyo. Although the Japanese war council did not know exactly when this assault would be, they commenced preparations for their ultimate stand to defend the Empire. Their operation was codenamed Ketsu-go. As part of Ketsu-go Kamikaze (suicide) planes, Kamikaze submarines, and manned torpedoes were stashed along the coastline where the Americans were suspected to land.[7] Japanese citizens were given instructions and in some cases training on how to fight American soldiers with household items and farming equipment. Each and every soldier and citizen was ready to fight to the bitter end and were ready to give their lives to defend the Emperor and the Empire.

President Truman knew there would be no surrender on the part of the Japanese, as they would quite literally rather die fighting in battle, then surrender to the enemy, for the former was seen as more honourable. His generals estimated that the campaign to conquer Japan would cause 1.7 million to 4 million casualties, including 800,000 deaths on the Americans side (all soldiers). They further estimated 5 million to 10 million Japanese deaths (soldiers and civilians). The number of human lives on the line was staggering.

President Truman was also aware of a new weapon in the U.S. arsenal that was so devastating, so violent, that it might actually get the Japanese to surrender and avoid the massacre to come. After the second bomb was dropped, the Emperor could not let his subjects suffer anymore. The Japanese Empire surrendered, avoiding the massacre of Operation Olympic/Ketsu-Go and the ensuing ground invasion altogether, saving more than 10 million lives. When President

---

[7]*After the Japanese surrender and ensuing peace, the Americans would discover that the Japanese Imperial army very accurately predicted where the American troops would land. It surely would have made for a scene far bloodier than D-Day.*

Truman ordered the deadliest and most violent bomb in human history to be dropped on unsuspecting civilians in Hiroshima and Nagasaki, he was doing the right thing and trying to save millions of lives. When given the option of executing 200,000 civilians to save the lives of more than 10 million human beings (both soldiers and civilians), a rational and logical person would most assuredly choose the lesser number of victims and therefore agree with the execution. This logic cannot be denied.

However, let the gravity of this moment in very recent history sink in for a moment. This is where you live. You live in a world where the inhumane massacre of hundreds of thousands of defenceless civilians is not only justifiable but sometimes the right thing to do. Take a moment, take a deep breath, close your eyes, and let the gravity of this dark situation sink in.

There simply is no justifiable reason to hurt any living being, let alone take a life. The world will tell you to divide and segregate, but this is wrong and hateful. Does divisiveness inspire tranquility? Does hate bring peace to your heart? Three billion heartbeats. *Tick tock.* How do you want to live the rest of your life?

There is no good reason for divisiveness and it is time we end it. Of course, *you* cannot go out there and end all the divisiveness in the world, but you can change *your* divisiveness. Separating people into groups based on nations, borders, religion, class, race, sex, etc. (the list goes on and on and on) are all forms of divisiveness. Any qualifier that creates a "We" and

"The Rest" scenario is wrong and hateful. You must never use any difference to segregate and divide. Note that you are not ignoring the differences between race, culture, sex, etc. The differences are there, and unique and beautiful to each group. However, you must see all 7.6 billion of us as a collective "WE." We are cosmopolitans, citizens of the planet Earth. Love everyone as equally as you love yourself. Why should your needs or your life be of any more importance than any other sentient beings?

Look up. Look at that blue sky and clouds, and remind yourself that it is an extremely thin sheet of air extending from you on the ground to the edge of space. The Earth is huge, right? Not really, only 12,742 km in diameter. If you drove straight through the planet to the other side at 100 km/h, it would take you more than five days to get to there. At first thought that may seem large; however, consider that all 7.6 billion of us live on this rock. There is nowhere else to go. In the vast universe that we have observed, all we have is this tiny rocky planet that is hurtling through space. Beyond that uncomfortably thin layer of atmosphere above your head, which is only 0.75% of the diameter of the already diminutive earth, is sheer, utter, unavoidable darkness. The vacuum of space is cold, uninhabitable, dark and unwelcoming. You have nowhere else to go. In the cosmic scale, planet Earth is tiny and you are marooned on it.

On December 7, 1972, the crew of the Apollo 17 spacecraft took the iconic picture known as *The Blue Marble* (above). Look at it. Look at that thin atmosphere (visible as the thin layer floating around the globe). Now look up at the sky and truly absorb and embrace the fear, fragility and small scale of this rocky planet we live on. Notice the background and surroundings. Black. Dark. Uninhabitable. This little rocky planet is all we have. It is the only thing all 7.6 billion of us have to live our brief lives on.

Remind yourself daily: Planet Earth is small, with no borders. We are all, we are one. See the world objectively and see all 7.6 billion as one. As brothers and sister. As friends. We live together. So let us begin to truly live together and not despite one another.

# 13 PHILOSOPHY AND THE PURSUIT OF KNOWLEDGE

The key to physical health is no secret: A healthy, varied whole food diet, and some physical activity. No need for complicated diets, no need for workout regiments. Eighty percent of physical health has to do with what goes in your mouth. The other twenty percent is to be active, to move around, hike, bike, mow the lawn etc. It does not necessarily mean hours spent at the gym. Keeping the physical body healthy can be very simple if one makes good choices. Seneca and Epictetus were quoted to go beyond the Stoic indifference towards physical exercise, and condemn anything beyond what is minimally necessary to keep the body in good health:

"But whatever you do, return from body to mind very soon."

- Lucius Annaeus Seneca

The key to mental health is also no secret. Much like diets and gym routines, we tend to overcomplicate mental health. The key to a tranquil life, as you know, is within you, as all you see, know and observe is subject to your judgment. This you know. The question becomes, how do you harden, train and improve your judgment? The answer is philosophy. Asking the right questions, reflecting on the basic questions of life, continuing to think about life, yourself, your surrounding and then meditating and reflecting on these is the only training regimen for your mind and inner dialogue. Philosophize until you become a philosopher king.

Question everything. Question everything you have heard, seen, observed and absorbed starting with everything in these collections of thoughts you are reading. Never take anything at base value, and never take anyone's words to be true simply because they are spoken. Remind yourself that you do not know what you do not know. This is a simple fact that most overlook. Know what you know, and be aware of and accept what you do not know. This, however, poses a conundrum: If you question things, and do not possess the knowledge to answer them yourself, then what do you do? Can you blindly rely on the words spoken by those who seem to know more than you do? The answer is a resounding no.

Therefore the pursuit of knowledge must go hand in hand with the pursuit of philosophy. Read and learn as much as you can. Read opposing ideas and texts. Listen to opposing ideas. See both sides to then find the right answer yourself.

"Look now, this is the starting point of philosophy: the recognition that different people have conflicting opinions, the rejection of mere opinion so that it comes to be viewed with mistrust, and investigation of opinion to determine whether it is rightly held, and the discovery of a standard of judgment, comparable to the balance that we have devised for the determining of weights, or the carpenter's rule for determining whether things are straight or crooked."

- Epictetus

And so, if you wish to have the capacity to question and answer for yourself and to philosophize on life and how to live it, you must arm yourself with the necessary tools – knowledge and a rational mind. There is nothing more important than the pursuit of knowledge and philosophy with a rational mind, and you must pursue them with vigour and discipline until the very last death, as this is a crucial necessity for a tranquil mind.

"As long as you live, keep learning how to live."

- Lucius Annaeus Seneca

# 14 NECESSITIES AND THE PURPOSE OF LIFE

The brilliant author Leo Tolstoy postulates at the end of his most famous novel and a work of art *War and Peace*, that everyone essentially wants the same thing: to be free. Free from burden and free from pain and suffering. He then points out that there is a direct and inverse relationship between freedom and necessities. He puts forth that the perception of necessity (needing or wanting something) creates the lack of perceived freedom. The more we need, the more we are burdened, the more we suffer from work, worry and anxiety, and therefore the less freedom we have from burden, pain and suffering.

If you consider the life Diogenes lived, tranquil and burden free, this certainly makes sense. After all, the universe ultimately demands very little of us. Food, water and sleep is all the universe absolutely require from us.[8] Therefore, anything you believe you need over and above these basic necessities is superficial, unnecessary and a construct of your own imagination. This imagination is often moulded by society, its "norms," marketing, etc. But it is still your own imagination nonetheless that decided what you think you need. You complicate your life for nothing and suffer the anxieties and work that comes with it for nothing. Do you need to travel? Do you need to buy more stuff? Do you need to make more money? Do you need more "glorified" titles? Do you need to eat fancy expensive foods, or drink fancy expensive drinks? Do you need a luxury car? Or three cars? Do you need to have a cloud-like bed to sleep on? Or a large house to sleep in?

> "As far as I am concerned, I know that I have lost not wealth but distractions. The body's needs are few: it wants to be free from cold, to banish hunger and thirst with nourishment; if we long for anything more we are exerting ourselves to serve our vices, not our needs."
>
> - Lucius Annaeus Seneca

---

[8] *One might argue that this is not taking into account the meteorological conditions of where one lives (i.e. if you live in a Nordic country, you would also require a shelter with a fireplace so as not to freeze to death). However, the universe does not prevent you from relocating to a more habitable climate, and so this "shelter and fire in a cold climate" is not a requirement imposed by the universe, but the individual's requirement from wanting to live in a climate that does not naturally support human life.*

Simplicity is one of the keys to a more free and tranquil life. The more simple the life, the fewer the needs and wants, the less work to attain it and upkeep it, and the less anxiety that comes with all of it. With respect to basic necessities, nature demands very little from you, and the more you want beyond that, the more complicated and stressful and less free your life becomes. This would explain why so many ancient philosophers were minimalists, to the point where some were even homeless by choice. Even the philosopher's cloak, which is so iconic of ancient philosophers and a symbol for wisdom in the modern world, was simply the minimum garment required for modesty and protection from the elements. (It is, after all, a simple piece of long fabric that is wrapped around the waist, with the extra bit flung over the shoulder.)

> "No person has the power to have everything they want, but it is in their power not to want what they do not have, and to cheerfully put to good use what they do have"
>
> - Lucius Annaeus Seneca

Clearly then, the physical basic necessities are little, and anything more is a distraction. But what about the spiritual basic necessities? Life is short and all is predetermined, however, the illusion of free will is all too real, and therefore you live and must continue to live as if you have free will. There is no other choice, no other reality, and we cannot "remember" the future even though it is predetermined, and so you must make choices with your perceived free will. But you ask yourself how do you make good choices? What are good choices? What is your guiding principle?

Your guiding principle of what is spiritually necessary for you must have to do with "what" you do here. But to answer the "what" you do here, you need to first answer "why" you are here. And so your guiding principle must necessarily be based on your purpose in life. Then what is the purpose of life to base this guiding principle on? Ultimately, what is the purpose of your life?

The universe always has, and always will do what it is going to do. There is no changing its will, no alternate reality where things are different. In order to have a tranquil life, one must accept what fate has, and will bestow upon them. Therefore the rational ordinary mind recognizes that a good guiding principle must be in line with the will of the universe. Put otherwise, your guiding principle must be in line with your purpose in life as defined and dictated by the universe.

The second law of thermodynamics states that when energy changes from one form to another form, or matter moves freely, entropy (disorder) in a closed system increases. We have observed this law in many systems, including the largest system known to us: The universe. The early universe appears to have been in thermal and chemical equilibrium[9] (also known as a low

---

[9] *The Cosmic Microwave Background (CMB) that was left over from the Big Bang is evenly distributed in all observable directions both in heat and chemistry. This means the early universe was in equilibrium and uniform throughout: a very low entropy state.*

entropy state), and yet today matter is scattered everywhere in an uneven manner. Things keep exploding, imploding, colliding and in general becoming more disordered. The universe is simply trying to reach the highest level of entropy it can. Therefore if you ask the magnificent universe what your purpose in life is, the simple answer is that the purpose of everything contained within it is to help the universe attain a higher level of entropy. More specifically, for you and all animal life on this planet, the purpose of life is to hydrogenate carbon dioxide.

Beyond this chemical reaction that takes in carbon dioxide (a lower entropy molecule) and turns it into methane amongst other compounds that get released through this reaction (a higher state of entropy), the universe has no other purpose for us. But do not feel snubbed by the universe, as this rule applies to everything else contained within it. Everything exists today because a higher level of entropy was reached from a lower one creating the matter we see. And everything that exists today will contribute to higher levels of entropy for the future.

So when you ask the almighty and magnificent universe what your purpose in life is, the answer is not only grossly underwhelming but also lacking. It is not enough as it is only concerned with the physical and ignores your need for a purpose in the conscious realm of your life. Fulfilling the universe's unbreakable three rules does not take the entirety of your time. Once you are rested, eaten and have had an adequate intake of water (all to fuel your body, the machine that hydrogenates carbon dioxide), you have all this spare time. Time spent conscious and self-aware. And so you need a purpose for your free, conscious and self-aware time. You need a spiritual purpose beyond the physical.

This means that your spiritual purpose in life that is beyond what the universe physically demands from you, must also come as a construct of your imagination as it transcends the physical. You must decide in your own mind what your purpose is. Ask yourself what your subjective needs are outside your objective reality? What is necessary for you to be happy and proud of your life? Is it the pursuit of money, power, titles, social gatherings, a devotion to a personalized god, becoming a positive agent for change, living in harmony with your environment, the pursuit of a tranquil life such that on your deathbed you can be at peace? Whatever it might be, it will be unique to every person, and so you must find your own spiritual basic necessities.

As you look inward for the answer regarding your purpose in life, do not rush it, and do not look for answers elsewhere. Getting external "recommendations" for a purpose will simply unduly influence you and keep you from identifying the true necessities you seek. Avoid outside influences, or at the very least do not follow them blindly. Once you find your true basic spiritual necessities (as identified objectively by yourself), you will be able to live your days in a type of harmony and peace you never felt before, as you will no longer have the feeling of fear that you are wasting your days or living life the wrong way.

To help you in your search for your unique spiritual basic necessities (referred to as necessities going forward for simplicity), here are some guidelines to follow:

1. You necessities must be decided on objectively. Question everything. Do not accept necessities that have been imposed on you by parents, preachers, society, television, school, Buddha, Seneca, anyone. You must define your necessities objectively, consciously and conscientiously.

2. As you evaluate your subjective needs, consider your objective reality. Make sure your necessities are realistic. You may want to help the starving children of Africa, however, due to logistics and finances, you simply cannot.

3. Every day is death, and any day could be your final death. Therefore, you must live your life day by day, as you die every day. If you want to be tranquil, you must be ready to die in peace any given day. *Memento Mori*. Given that fulfilling our necessities should be granting you peace of mind on your deathbed, your necessities cannot be set out to accomplish something in the future. A necessity, therefore, must be something that can be accomplished daily.

4. Your necessities are yours. You must be able to accomplish them should you chose to, regardless of external factors. Therefore they cannot be linked to fate and the universes will. It cannot be related to anything external to you including loved ones, careers or materials. They must be internal, under your

control, which means they must be 100% subject to *only* your judgment, choices, and actions.

5. You must periodically re-evaluate your necessities as they may, on occasion, change over time. If, however, they change too often, you have not identified your true necessities. True necessities will be deeply rooted within you, touching back to your core ethics, morals and values. If your core is rapidly changing, that means they are superficial and that you are distracting yourself as you are still afflicted from not having found your true necessities.

6. Make a list of your old necessities and keep them right next to your new ones. When you write down and see what you used to live for in the past, it will remind you what you do not want to be and the falsehoods you used to believe in. This will help you better identify your necessities and stay in compliance with them.

As a point of clarification, you may, and should have long-term goals, if they fit with your necessities. However, if you do, remind yourself that the human effort is not entirely efficient. So long-term goals might work out or might not. As hard as you try, there will always be more variables controlled by the universe than you. And so do not live by your goals and measure success based on their outcomes. Measure success on your moral good, on whether you set out to do what you objectively, consciously and conscientiously identified as your necessities.

With your necessities identified and written down, the direction becomes clear and the rules of engagement defined. Now go live that good life one day at a time and make the good choices.

"He who has a why to live for can bear almost any how."

- Friedrich Nietzsche

# 15 THE PURSUIT OF A TRANQUIL LIFE

The pursuit of a tranquil life is a lifelong journey. In general philosophers, both ancient and modern, believe that one must live for oneself, as there is no other divine purpose. To be clear, this does not mean "if it makes you happy and does not hurt anyone, then do it." Attaining happiness – or rather the pursuit of it – is no different than any other distraction, a mere vice.

"Vices have to be crushed rather than picked at."

- Lucius Annaeus Seneca

One must live for oneself, meaning to live for their self-identified necessities. You cannot chase distractions or vices all the time, but you can have a tranquil state of mind all the time, regardless of what is happening in your life. Therefore living for yourself necessarily means, live in a way to have and lead a tranquil life. Live in a manner such that it makes you proud.

Live, as the Stoic will say, in the way of life of an ideal good man.

> "Waste no more time arguing what a good man should be. Be One."
>
> - Marcus Aurelius

Simplicity and virtue should be core values. Simplify your life in every way, from diet, to duties, to material goods, to goals, to objectives, etc. Simplify all dimensions of your life. Simplicity will help you avoid unnecessary anxieties and give you more freedom of mind, body, and soul. Simplify your "wants" to the only things you control: Your judgments and actions. Want to have good judgments and actions, nothing more.

Virtue will also fend off unnecessary and self-inflicted angst, anxiety and Consternation, as to be virtue requires honesty, honourability, and rational thought.

Honesty, not only simplifies life but avoids all the angst, anxiety and afflictions that dishonesty always foster's. It is better not to say anything on the subject matter than to tell a lie. Do not lie to anyone, especially not to yourself. To be honourable, you must be fair, compassionate, polite, brave and above all never put your needs over that of another. Your needs are no more important than any other single sentient being, and so behave in a manner reflective of this truth. Being honourable will give you the peace of mind and love of oneself, and will avoid all tormented feelings that come with behaving in a decrepit manner. Rational thought will ensure that you view the world as it is, objectively and always make the best possible decisions regardless of what is going on around you externally. Do not be so proud that you view yourself to be better than others. You are unique but are not special or more important or deserving than any of your brothers and sisters on planet Earth. Your rational ordinary mind knows to love all sentient beings.

Reject with disgust all divisiveness based on any grounds as your rational ordinary mind knows all sentient beings are equal, both in the eyes of the universe and in yours. You will be virtuous, others may not be, but still, both your needs and lives are equally important. And so treat them with compassion, even if they don't respond in kind. Be honest with the world and most importantly be honest with yourself.

> "Above all, don't lie to yourself. The man who lies to himself and listens to his own lie comes to a point that he cannot distinguish the truth within him, or around him, and so loses all respect for himself and for others. And having no respect he ceases to love."
>
> - Fyodor Dostoyevsky

Do not present yourself as the person you wish others to see you, just be you, be happy with you and be honest in all respects, as this is simple and tranquil.

"If anyone tells you that a certain person speaks ill of you, do not make excuses about what is said of you but answer, 'He was ignorant of my other faults, else he would not have mentioned these alone.' "

- Epictetus

Do not be a preacher. You are living your life for yourself, not to educate others. You are pursuing a life of tranquility, not a life of trying to educate the people. Trying to give advice or opinions to people who do not want to hear them, disagree with them, or worse applaud and cheer them for the sake of social decorum will bring angst and afflictions along with them. Worst of all, your precious finite time would be wasted.

If, however, you are approached for opinions or teachings, then you must help your fellow being. If you have been requested to educate, then you have a listening ear. A listening ear will take your teachings to heart and become a better person, thus making the world a better place. Therefore, your duty is to educate when asked to do so by a listening ear. Otherwise, do not preach to non-listeners or crowds. Your precious time should not be wasted and should be spent pursuing a tranquil life.

"Do not explain your philosophy. Embody it."

- Epictetus

The pursuit of philosophy and knowledge should never stop. At all times, if you are not answering one of the few demands of the universe, you should be pursuing philosophy and knowledge with an insatiable haste, spending as much of your time as you can learning, reflecting, philosophizing.

Live by your necessities. Your new found, objective basic spiritual necessities.

Declutter the mind regularly. Write down your thoughts and make difficult decisions on paper to ensure you are using the most rational ordinary mind.

Remind yourself of Marcus Aurelius' three rules for a tranquil and good life:

1. Discipline of judgment – Things are as you see them, so make sure you see them rationally and objectively. Things do not affect you. Your judgment of things affect you.

2. Discipline of action – All that you say and do is always after the fact. Choose your responses and reactions such that they are virtuous, compassionate, and that they fit with your necessities.

3. Discipline of the consent to Destiny – The Universe is going to do what it does and you quite literally have no choice in the matter. When "bad" things happen, they are not actually bad. They just are. There is no fair, unfair, good, or bad because this would imply the existence of another reality where things happened differently, and that you can go to that reality. There is just the one reality, this one, and you cannot change it, so just go the way things are.

Avoid all emotions. Feel them if you must, however never let them get behind the wheel and take control of how you live. Emotions, good or bad, come and go. Your rational ordinary mind remains, and therefore even when swept by emotions your rational ordinary mind should be in the driver's seat while making judgments of the external world, as viewed by your mind.

All the principles listed above are not like computer program, which is applied once and systematically and automatically triggered in all situations going forward. No, the practice of the above principles is instead a sort of awakening of the mind and spirit to a new life, a better life, one filled with tranquility. However, this awakening is quick to disappear, so you must meditate on all of these on a daily basis. Find creative ways to repeat them. Write them down. Twice a day. Read them back. Twice a day. Read and re-read these pages periodically. Sit in a place with no distractions and think only about these rules. Each time you write or read or meditate on them, you will take one more step towards becoming a philosopher king.

Like the 33 miners who were trapped underground for 69 days, so many others who have had a brush with death drastically changed their approach to life after getting a "second chance." They changed their lives for the better with clearer views of what is truly important and adapted proper morals and necessities to truly enjoy, and make the most of this one finite and precious life we get. Do not wait for a near-death experience to realize the priorities in life and begin living the right way. Live it now, there is no second turn around and everyday time passes us by. Do not wait until old age revelations, or an accident to change your approach to life. What's left of your 3 billion heartbeats? How do you want to spend it? *Tick tock.*

# ABOUT THE AUTHOR

After many years of misery, stress and search for meaning, ANDERSON SILVER through study, reflection and meditations found a tranquility he never thought possible. Periodically, Anderson shared some of his meditations with people around him having spiritual breakdowns, who also found inner peace through these thoughtful reflections. From this experience arose Your User's Manual, which aims to help readers obtain the tranquility and purpose that we all seek. A graduate of Concordia University, today Anderson is a CPA, a husband, and father of three. He resides in Montreal. Your User's Manual is his first book.